CANADA'S MODERN-DAY FIRST NATIONS

Nunavut and Evolving Relationships

TITLE LIST

CANADA'S MODERN-DAY FIRST NATIONS

Nunavut and Evolving Relationships

BY
ELLYN SANNA WITH WILLIAM HUNTER

MASON CREST PUBLISHERS
PHILADELPHIA

Mason Crest Publishers Inc.
370 Reed Road
Broomall, Pennsylvania 19008
(866) MCP-BOOK (toll free)

First printing
1 2 3 4 5 6 7 8 9 10

Library of Congress Cataloging-in-Publication Data

Library of Congress Cataloging-in-Publication Data

Sanna, Ellyn, 1958–
   Canada's modern-day First Nations : Nunavut and evolving relationships
/ by Ellyn Sanna with William Hunter.
      p. cm. — (How Canada became Canada)
   Includes bibliographical references and index.
   ISBN 1-4222-0010-8   ISBN 1-4222-0000-0 (series)
   1. Inuit—Nunavut—History. 2. Inuit—Nunavut—Politics and government.
3. Inuit—Nunavut—Social life and customs. 4. Self-determination, National
—Nunavut. 5. Nunavut—History. 6. Nunavut—Politics and government.
I. Hunter, William, 1971–   . II. Title. III. Series: Sanna, Ellyn, 1958–   .
How Canada became Canada.
E99.E7S318 2006
971.9'500497124—dc22
                                                2005014804

Produced by Harding House Publishing Service, Inc.
www.hardinghousepages.com
Interior design by MK Bassett-Harvey.
Cover design by Dianne Hodack.
Printed in the Hashemite Kingdom of Jordan.

CONTENTS

INTRODUCTION

by David Bercuson

Every country's history is distinct, and so is Canada's. Although Canada is often said to be a pale imitation of the United States, it has a unique history that has created a modern North American nation on its own path to democracy and social justice. This series explains how that happened.

Canada's history is rooted in its climate, its geography, and in its separate political development. Virtually all of Canada experiences long, dark, and very cold winters with copious amounts of snowfall. Canada also spans several distinct geographic regions, from the rugged western mountain ranges on the Pacific coast to the forested lowlands of the St. Lawrence River Valley and the Atlantic tidewater region.

Canada's regional divisions were complicated by the British conquest of New France at the end of the Seven Years' War in 1763. Although Britain defeated France, the French were far more numerous in Canada than the British. Britain was thus forced to recognize French Canadian rights to their own language, religion, and culture. That recognition is now enshrined in the Canadian Constitution. It has made Canada a democracy that values group rights alongside individual rights, with official French/English bilingualism as a key part of the Canadian character.

During the American Revolution, Canadians chose to stay British. After the Revolution, they provided refuge to tens of thousands of Americans who, for one reason or another, did not follow George Washington, Benjamin Franklin, or the other founders of the United States who broke with Britain.

Democracy in Canada under the British Crown evolved more slowly than it did in the United States. But in the early nineteenth century, slavery was outlawed in the

British Empire, and as a result, also in Canada. Thus Canada never experienced civil war or government-imposed racial segregation.

From these few, brief examples, it is clear that Canada's history differs considerably from that of the United States. And yet today, Canada is a true North American democracy in its own right. Canadians will profit from a better understanding of how their country was shaped—and Americans may learn much about their own country by studying the story of Canada.

The frozen waters of the far north

One
FIRST NATIONS' PLACE IN CANADA'S IDENTITY

Long ago, groups of people from the icy land of what is now Siberia set off on a long journey. These explorers and colonizers of a new land traveled across the land bridge that once connected the continents of Asia and North America. Slowly, with their babies and all their belongings strapped on their backs, the people ventured farther and farther east. They hunted the great wooly mammoths that wandered the land; the huge animals provided them with meat, and they used the hides and bones to make their tents, clothing, and tools. They were a strong people, used to surviving in a cold, harsh climate, and they knew how to live in harmony with their mother the Earth. Some of them moved south, and gradually they spread across the entire continent of North America and then still farther south, down through South America. These people formed the Americas' first nations. They were also the founding mothers and fathers of the land that is now Canada.

Millennia later, when Europeans moved into Canada's wide open lands, they encountered these First Nations, just as the American colonists did to the south. Many of the same conflicts arose in Canada as in the United States, as the two groups of people were forced to live side by side. People of European descent often failed to see the value of First Nations cultures; many white people considered First Nations to be

What Does the Term "First Nations" Mean?

Many terms have been used to refer to the Native people of North America. In Canada today, these people are usually called First Nations, because they literally lived in Canada first, thousands of years before Europeans or anyone else arrived. Other terms used to describe First Nations people include:

Indian—Christopher Columbus thought he had reached India when he landed in the Americas in 1492. For centuries, people continued to call the Native North Americans Indians. Canada's official laws still refer to the First Nations as Indians.

Aboriginal people—Aboriginal means "existing from the beginning." The Canadian Constitution recognizes three groups of Aboriginal people—Indians, Métis, and Inuit—three separate peoples with unique heritages, languages, cultural practices, and spiritual beliefs.

Native Canadians—This term was suggested to parallel the U.S. usage of Native Americans, but it never really caught on.

An early Inuit

First Nations woman

primitive, uneducated, and savage. Few Europeans understood Native religious beliefs or values, and most whites considered their own society and beliefs to be superior to First Nations'. Meanwhile, First Nations lacked the technology and scientific advantages that would have allowed them to compete on an equal footing with the white newcomers. When disputes over land arose, the First Nations were often the losers.

Unlike the United States, however, Canada was never completely infiltrated by the European settlers. Vast reaches of land to the north remained unsettled and unspoiled by white civilization. While Americans resolved their land conflicts by moving Native groups to reservations, many Canadian Natives were able to simply move away from the white settlements. Those who had always lived in the cold northern lands continued to live their lives just as their ancestors had for thousands of years before them.

These people of the far north were once referred to as Eskimos, a Native word that may have meant "she who laces a snowshoe"—or perhaps "eater of raw meat." They had their own names for themselves, however: Inuit, Yupik, and Inupiat. All these

First Nations Groups

Many different First Nations groups besides the Inuit live across Canada. Some of these include:

Cree	Diné (Navajo)	Haida	Iskut
Innu	Ojibwe	Mi'kmaq	Algonquin
Iroquois	Wendat (Huron)	Dakota	Tlingit

Native words mean "the Real People," and today, the word "Eskimo" is no longer used. These people have lived in the Arctic reaches of Canada for more than four thousand years.

At first, in the early years after the Real People met the European newcomers in the seventeenth century, Native life changed very little. In the eighteenth century, however, as more and more Europeans ventured

The Métis

One of the largest First Nations groups in Canada is the Métis, a group descended from European fur traders and Native women. As the children of mixed ancestry increased in number, they in turn married among themselves, and eventually they developed a new culture, neither European nor Native but a fusion of the two. With their command of both European and Native languages and cultures, the Métis often acted as intermediaries when the two cultures did business. The Métis people also played a major role in Canada's formation as a nation, and today, the Métis people continue to work for the recognition and justice they deserve, specifically in relation to land rights.

The Métis Nation's Homeland is based on the traditional territory where the Métis people have historically lived within west central North America, which includes Manitoba, Alberta, and Saskatchewan; parts of Ontario, British Columbia, and the Northwest Territories; as well as parts of the northern United States (North Dakota and Montana). It is estimated that there are 350,000 to 400,000 Métis Nation citizens in Canada; they represent 26 percent of the total First Nations population in Canada.

Inuit woman

Alien Invasion

Imagine how human life would change if we were forced to share the Earth with aliens from another planet. These newcomers would bring with them new technologies, new materials, new tools, and perhaps most important, new ways of thinking about life. As a result, the most ordinary details of our lives would eventually be radically changed in ways we can't even imagine. The situation faced by the Real People of the North was very similar to this science-fiction scenario.

further north, first as whalers and then as fur traders, Native culture was forced to adapt to a series of new pressures, opportunities, and values. The objects of their daily life began to be made in different ways from different materials: wood replaced bone; iron and copper replaced stone; and woven fabrics replaced skins. Nails and needles revolutionized the way they built their boats and made their clothing. New weapons

Inuit settlement

changed the way they hunted and defended themselves.

Some of the changes brought by the Europeans were positive, but many were not. Whalers destroyed huge numbers of animals, endangering an important source of Native food, and as fur trappers moved into the area, they brought with them a new economy based on practices that eroded the traditional Native social groups. The traditions of the Real People were based on cooperation, sharing, and a sense of responsibility to one another—but they had to learn about competition and independence if they

Inuit clad in sealskin parkas

were to survive in the new world the white men created.

Microscopic organisms caused one of the most tragic effects of the European invasion—and white people didn't even know they carried them. The Real People had no immunity to the germs that were commonplace in Europe, and as a result, thousands of people died. Some white people wondered if the Real People might disappear altogether. An explorer who visited Frobisher Bay in 1861 wrote: "The days of the Inuit are numbered. There are very few of them left now. Fifty years may find them all passed away, without leaving one to tell that such a people ever lived." A missionary living in

17

Cumberland Sound a few years later agreed: "The extermination of the whole Eskimo population . . . is only a matter of time."

Fortunately, these predictions did not come true. Disease took a terrible toll on the Real People of the North, but they proved to be strong and resourceful enough to survive, despite the enormous challenges they faced. In many ways, they learned to incorporate the changes they faced into the fabric of their lives. First Nations people had a long heritage of courage and hardiness, and this stood them in good stead.

One example of this is the way in which First Nations integrated Christianity's symbols and practices with Native faith and rituals. In many ways, European missionaries carried cultural change with them along with their Bibles—and yet these people of faith also acted as *advocates* for First Nations, speaking up for them against the greed

A modern-day Inuit Christian church incorporates traditional Native concepts into its architecture.

18

of whalers, trappers, and land-hungry whites. What's more, the missionaries translated Christian terms into Native words that already held deep spiritual meaning, and the church incorporated many traditional Native rituals so that they took on Christian meaning as well. Some First Nations groups came to believe that Native religions had anticipated Christian teachings, that Christianity fulfilled rather than negated their ancient traditions.

A modern-day First Nations individual has this to say about Native Christianity:

> We often hear non-Inuit talk about how missionaries were not good for us. When Inuit talk about this, they usually give another opinion and tell of their respect for the religious teachings, and for the other roles they played especially in those early days. Some have recently turned to more fundamental religions while individuals continue to stay with the churches of their childhood. One way or another these teachings have become part of our life and culture.

The white newcomers to Canada's ancient land brought with them change and new ideas—and their culture was in

Advocates are people who speak out or act in support of something.

19

Federalism is a form of government in states, provinces, or regions that defers certain powers to a central government while retaining a limited measure of self-government.

turn transformed by its contact with First Nations people. Long before the first European settlers crossed the Atlantic, Canada's original inhabitants had a rich culture based on respect for the earth and all forms of life, and these vibrant and practical values enriched Canada's formation. The early settlers from Europe might not even have survived in their "New World" if not for the help and support of Canada's First Nations, who taught the newcomers how to live in a harsh natural environment. In eastern Canada, the Iroquois's government was so sophisticated that it served as a model for Canada's concept of *federalism*. First Nations shared their values and knowledge, played active roles in Canada's journey toward Confederation, and helped create the modern nation Canada has become today.

First Nations' Important Role in Canada's History

During the nineteenth-century wars with the United States, Indian forces helped protect their country's borders from persistent invasions from the south. The Métis of the Northwest laid the foundation for the creation of the Province of Manitoba and its subsequent entry into the Confederation. What's more, it was the Métis who insisted on Manitoba's federation with Canada and resisted American annexation policies.

A First Nations totem pole on the streets of Ottawa, Canada's capital city.

Unfortunately, not all Canadians have recognized First Nations' vital role in their nation's growth. First Nations people endured centuries of conflict and destruction. Today, however, some Canadian historians speak of their country's story as a house supported by three pillars: the French, the English, and the First Nations. In the past, many Canadians tried to tell the story without the First Nations' pillar, leaving Native people outside Canada's sheltering roof— but now it is time to "extend the rafters" (an Iroquois metaphor) and accept that Canada's house cannot be complete unless all three pillars are acknowledged and valued.

The Canadian government has issued this statement of reconciliation, spelling out the debt owed to First Nations while affirming their place in modern Canada:

The assistance and spiritual values of the Aboriginal peoples who welcomed the newcomers to this continent too often have been forgotten. The contributions made by all Aboriginal peoples to Canada's development, and the contributions that they continue to make to our society today, have not been properly acknowledged. The Government of Canada today, on behalf of all Canadians, acknowledges those contributions.

Sadly, our history with respect to the treatment of Aboriginal people is not something in which we can take pride. Attitudes of racial and cultural superiority led to a suppression of Aboriginal culture and values. As a country, we are burdened by past actions that resulted in weakening the identity of Aboriginal peoples, suppressing their languages and cultures, and outlawing spiritual practices. We must recognize the impact of

Canada's "house"—government buildings in Ottawa—is built on three pillars: the French, the English, and the

these actions on the once self-sustaining nations that were disaggregated, disrupted, limited or even destroyed by the dispossession of traditional territory, by the relocation of Aboriginal people, and by some provisions of the Indian Act. We must acknowledge that the result of these actions was the erosion of the political, economic and social systems of Aboriginal people and nations.

Against the backdrop of these historical legacies, it is a remarkable tribute to the strength and endurance of Aboriginal people that they have maintained their historic diversity and identity. The Government of Canada today formally expresses to all Aboriginal people in Canada our profound regret

for past actions of the federal government which have contributed to these difficult pages in the history of our relationship together. . . .

Reconciliation is an ongoing process. In renewing our partnership, we must ensure that the mistakes which marked our past relationship are not repeated. The Government of Canada recognizes that policies that sought to assimilate Aboriginal people, women and men, were not the

An Inuit elder

A modern-day Inuit woman and her grandchild

way to build a strong country. We must instead continue to find ways in which Aboriginal people can participate fully in the economic, political, cultural and social life of Canada in a manner which preserves and enhances the collective identities of Aboriginal communities, and allows them to evolve and flourish in the future. Working together to achieve our shared goals will benefit all Canadians, Aboriginal and non-Aboriginal alike.

The ideals expressed in this statement are the goals toward which Canada is working. History cannot be undone or erased, but as Canadians acknowledge the issues involved with justice for First Nations, they can find new and better ways to move together toward the future. One of the biggest and most complicated of these issues has to do with Native land claims.

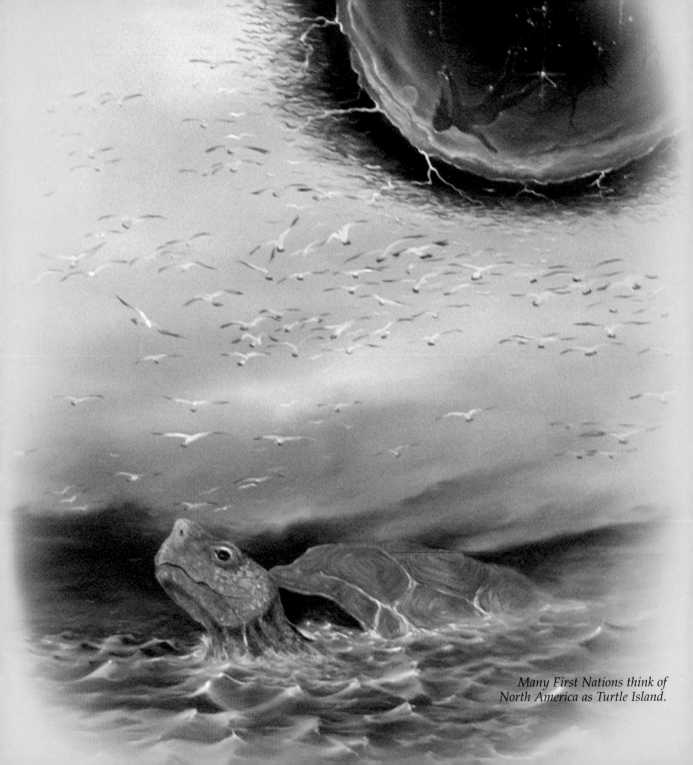

Many First Nations think of North America as Turtle Island.

Two
LAND CLAIMS AND OTHER CONTROVERSIES

When the white-skinned Europeans crossed the Atlantic Ocean, they called the land they found the "New World"—but for the people who already lived in the Americas, their world was so old that it connected them with the very beginnings of Creation. Many First Nations groups thought of North America as Turtle Island, a huge piece of land that formed on the back of an enormous turtle after the first woman fell from the sky. The Real People flourished on Turtle Island. They drew their life and their identity from its soil, and they valued it and honored it as though it were their mother.

The arrival of the Europeans broke this intimate connection between the land and the people who lived on it. The newcomers did not regard the Earth as their mother; instead, they saw the land as something to be broken into pieces and owned.

In the late nineteenth and early twentieth centuries, many First Nations groups signed treaties with representatives of the British Crown. These treaties did not mean the same thing to the First Nations as they did to the Europeans. The British believed the treaties gave them complete control over the land, making it safe for settlement and for the development of its resources; they considered that the treaties transferred the

*A **title** is a document giving the legal right to a property.*

land's **title** to them. Meanwhile, the First Nations perceived the treaties as agreements between two groups to share the land, in the same way the First Nations shared it with the animals and each other. First Nations people had strong concepts of territory, but they did not believe land was something an individual could divide, transfer, surrender, destroy, or own. These thoughts were so strange to their way of thinking that it never even occurred to them that white people could look at things so differently.

In the conflict between cultures, First Nations people struggled to maintain their relationship with the land. According to some thinkers, the most basic right of all human

Native Views of the Land

"Our land is more valuable than your money. It will last forever. It will not even perish by the flames of fire. As long as the sun shines and the waters flow, this land will be here to give life to men and animals. It was put here by the Great Spirit and we cannot sell it because it does not belong to us."

"Sell a country! Why not sell the air, the clouds and the great sea, as well as the earth? Did not the great spirit make them all for the use of his children?"

Traditional sculpture in modern-day First Nations legislative assembly

beings is their right to their own unique identity—and for the First Nations, that identity was built on the land where they lived before the arrival of Europeans.

In the twentieth century, First Nations groups began actively working to reclaim their heritage. Canadian First Nations might not have understood the concept of land ownership when they first encountered Europeans, but today First Nations believe they had—and still have—certain rights to the land where they lived. These include the right to live on their ancestral lands, to use it for hunting, fishing, trapping, gathering food and medicines, and any other traditional activities.

First Nations leaders clarify that the right to identity also implies the right to *self-determination*, for it is through self-determination that they will be able to preserve their identity as a group. According to First Nations people, when the Earth is *exploited* and abused, as happens when a hydroelectric project, a pipeline, or a strip mine destroys natural resources, the traditional ways First Nations support themselves are disrupted or damaged. That's why when First Nations assert their land rights, they include the trees and animals; the rivers, hills, and coastal waters; the ice, the air, and the resources beneath the soil.

All these things, they insist, are integral parts of their Mother the Earth. Aboriginal people also speak of their "*collective* and *inalienable right*" to the land. Land, as they see it, is not something to be bought and sold, but something for which the entire community is responsible, which must be passed on to future generations. The land offers them more than just the means to make a living and support themselves: it is also a place where the spirits of their ancestors live and where their children and children's children will grow up.

First Nations see the Earth as their mother.

In 1876, the Canadian government passed the Indian Act, which spelled out its responsibility to the First Nations and their lands through treaty making. Despite this formal commitment, the government has not always honored its legal obligations under the Indian Act or the treaties that preceded

***Self-determination** is the right of people to determine a form of government without outside interference.*

*To be **exploited** is to be used or taken advantage of.*

***Collective** means shared by everyone in a group.*

*An **inalienable right** is a right that cannot be transferred or taken away.*

Inuit legislative assembly

and followed it. In most cases, the government did not provide the full amount of land promised under treaty.

Today, First Nations people believe the treaties they signed with the British government are nothing more than a series of broken promises. What's more, many First Nations groups never signed a treaty. Much of the Canadian landmass where First Nations people lived for centuries before the coming of the Europeans was never officially given away. As a result, many First Nations are now seeking the return of their land—or compensation for what was taken from them—in the courts, from Parliament, and through land claims negotiations.

As they pursue these land claims, First Nations work toward a range of opportunities. In some cases, they may ask that fishing and hunting be locally managed and controlled in accordance with traditional Native values. In other cases, they may seek a share in the profits from large industries such as logging, commercial fishing, and mining. In all land claims, the goal is to provide the means that will allow First Nations to prosper and grow—culturally, economically, spiritually, and socially—in ways denied to them in the past. Land claims seek to accomplish this goal while affirming First Nations' sense of community and identity.

Some of these grievances go back a hundred years or more. Settling a claim with the government is a long process, and claims are accepted for negotiation only when it is determined that Canada has an outstanding "lawful obligation" to a First Nation. Today, there are more than 450 outstanding specific land claims filed with the federal govern-

ment, but only 140 or so are actually in the process of negotiation. Many other claims have been rejected.

In the summer of 1991, a national crisis erupted over one of these rejected land claims. A group of Mohawk Indians barricaded a section of forest in Oka, near Montréal, after the town council won an appeal to build a golf course on part of the Mohawks' sacred burial grounds. The Mohawks declared war, and a policeman was killed in a shoot-out. The siege lasted all

Fishing is regarded as essential to many First Nations' identities.

33

Nunavut's official seal

summer, sparking a countrywide debate on First Nations' land rights.

Canada's government responded by setting up the Indian Claims Commission to study cases that have been rejected for negotiation by the government, an independent body that provides recommendations to the government. Since then, six previously rejected claims have been settled, and over twenty others have been accepted for negotiation.

With First Nations spread across the country, however, each having its own individual specific claim, they are often unable to sustain sufficient pressure to achieve positive and speedy action on any particular claim. Meanwhile, government resources for settling land claims are scarce. Despite major land claims agreements such as the James Bay and Northern Quebec Agreement, the Northern Flood Agreement in Manitoba, and the Umbrella Final Agreement in the Yukon, it will likely be decades before most treaty obligations are finally honored.

However, in 1993, the largest land claim in Canadian history led to a major success story for the Real People of the Northwest Territories—and the formation of a new Canadian territory.

Nunavut, "our land"

Three

THE FORMATION OF NUNAVUT

Nunavut means "our land," the land belonging to the Real People of Canada's far north. This vast territory stretches across some 733,594 square miles (1.9 million square kilometers). That's nearly one-fifth of Canada's entire area.

The Inuit originally presented their land claim to the federal government in 1976, but for years, negotiations made little progress. Then, in 1982, the Tungavik Federation of Nunavut (TFN) assumed the negotiating role on behalf of the Inuit, and things began to move slowly forward. After eight years, the TFN, the government of the Northwest Territories, and the government of Canada finally *ratified* and signed an agreement-in-principle (AIP) in 1990. (An AIP contains the basic elements of a final agreement but is not legally binding.) After the Inuit ratified the AIP, a final agreement needed to be reached. On May 25, 1993, the Nunavut Land Claims Agreement was signed in the city of Iqaluit.

The agreement is considered to be one of the most *innovative* agreements ever reached between a government and a group of Aboriginal people. It gives the Inuit ownership,

Ratified means officially approved.

If something is *innovative*, it is new and original or takes an original approach.

Nunavut children

rights, and obligations for the land, water, and resources of Nunavut. The Inuit also received $1.14 billion payable over a fourteen-year period ending in 2007. A $13 million training trust fund ensured the Inuit had access to sufficient training dollars to enable them to meet their responsibilities. As well, Inuit became full participants in a number of agencies responsible for the careful management of the territory's resources.

Features of the Nunavut Land Claims Agreement

Some of the more outstanding of the agreement's forty-one articles include:

- Equal representation of the Inuit on a new set of wildlife management, resource management, and environmental boards.

- The right to harvest wildlife on lands and waters throughout the Nunavut settlement area.

- A share of federal government royalties for Nunavut Inuit from oil, gas, and mineral development on government lands.

- Where Inuit own the surface title to the land, the right to negotiate with industry for economic and social benefits with nonrenewable resource development.

- The right of first refusal on sport and commercial development of renewable resources in the Nunavut Settlement Area.

- The creation of three federally funded national parks.

Stone monument in Nunavut

- The inclusion of a political accord that provided for the establishment of the new Territory of Nunavut and through this a form of self-government for the Nunavut Inuit.

*A **plebiscite** is a vote by a whole electorate to decide a question of importance.*

Nunavut Territory

The final agreement also included the Canadian government's promise to recommend to Parliament legislation that would establish a Nunavut Territory. A **plebiscite** to confirm the boundary between the old Northwest Territories and the new territory took place in May 1992. On April 1, 1999, Nunavut became Canada's newest and largest territory.

The creation of Nunavut Territory means the Inuit now have a form of self-government since they comprise approximately 85 percent of the territory's population. With their majority represented in the territory's government, they have the chance to pursue their goals and cultural values through a public government structure.

The government of Nunavut incorporates Inuit values and beliefs into a modern system of government. The working

The Nunavut Flag

The blue and gold symbolize the riches of the land, sea, and sky. Red indicates the connection to Canada as a whole. The *inukshuk* (stone monument) stands for that which guides the people and marks what is sacred. The star is the *Niqirtsuituq*, the North Star, the traditional guide for navigation, which also symbolizes the leadership of the community's elders.

language is Inuktitut (although English and French are also used). Each department has an Inuit Employment Plan to increase the number of Inuit in public service to levels that reflect their proportion of the population. As well, a number of departments are involved in preserving and promoting Inuit culture and values. These cultural values are reflected in everything from Nunavut school curriculum to conservation.

On the day of Nunavut's official birth as a territory, the Real People began their

Nunavut's flag

41

journey into the future by honoring centuries of tradition. People sang and danced and drummed. Paul Okalik, Nunavut's new premier, spoke with emotion: "Today the people of Nunavut formally join Canada.

Today we stand strong and we welcome the changes Nunavut brings."

His inauguration into office ended with a "communion of arrival," a traditional Inuit ceremony that marks the end of a long jour-

The Nunavut Coat of Arms

The dominant colors of blue and gold symbolize the riches of the land, sea, and sky. At the base of the shield, the inukshuk stands for that which guides the people and marks what is sacred. The *qulliq*, or Inuit stone lamp, represents light and the warmth of family and the community. The concave arc of the five gold circles refers to the life-giving properties of the sun arching above and below the horizon. The star is the Niqirtsuituq, the North Star, which is the traditional guide for navigation. The igloo represents the traditional life of the people and their means of survival. The Royal Crown symbolizes public government for all people of Nunavut and establishes Nunavut as a partner in the Confederation. The *tuktu* (caribou) and *qilalugaq tugaalik* (narwhal) refer to the land and sea animals that are part of Nunavut's natural heritage. The base of the crest is composed of land and sea and features three species of Arctic wildflowers. The motto in Inuktitut—*Nunavut Sanginivut*—means "Nunavut, our strength."

ney. Everyone present was handed glasses of water from all sections of Nunavut and a small bite of food.

"Let us celebrate the journey's end," said an Inuit elder who attended.

The journey that led to this day brought the Real People through centuries of challenge and change. Along the way, they had never lost sight of what was truly important to them. This sense of vision gave them

Nunavut's future

Nunavut Coat of Arms

hope and made them strong—and now it would lead them forward into a new journey, with their role in Canada officially recognized at last.

Iqaluit, Nunavut's capital city

Four
DAILY LIFE IN NUNAVUT AND OTHER
FIRST NATIONS COMMUNITIES

For many people, Nunavut seems like a faraway place. It's hard for them to imagine what life is like for the people who live there.

If you were to pay a visit to Iqaluit, the capital city of Nunavut, you would take a plane, since no roads connect the territory with the land to the south. The first thing you might notice as you got off the plane would probably be the cold. On a fall day in early November, the temperature would be around 5° Fahrenheit (–15°C). With the wind-chill factor, the air will feel more like –13° (–25°C), and snow might sting your face as you leave the airport.

As you wander around the city, you might be surprised to see the people you pass aren't bundled up against the cold. Plenty of people make their way along the streets of Iqaluit, and they're well acclimated to the temperature. Walking along the street, you also notice wolf pelts and sealskins stretched on a few of the fences. Although Iqaluit is a modern city, many people still follow the traditional patterns of life, earning their living in harmony with the Earth's cycles. In November, Frobisher Bay is already starting to freeze, which means people can walk out on the water to hunt seal.

If you stop for a bite to eat in a restaurant, the steep prices might give you another surprise—until you consider that almost every item of food on the menu must be flown in from the south. No farming takes place on Nunavut's icy land. Those who live there depend on seal, polar bear, and caribou for their meat.

As you eat, you might be approached several times by young people with homemade crafts to sell. Making knit goods, stone carvings, and art prints keeps young adults occupied during the long, dark winters, while helping to ground them in the traditions of their people. What's more, it brings in an income for their families. Some young adults may commute back and forth between remote areas and the capital city,

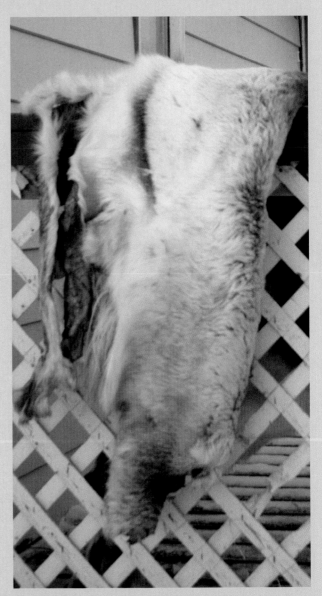

Wolf pelt hanging from an Iqaluit fence

Nunavut Fast Facts

Capital city: Iqaluit (population 4,500)

Total population: 25,000 (Inuit make up 85 percent of this total)

Number of people per 100 square kilometers: 1.3 (compared to 29 for Canada as a whole)

Percentage of population under 25: 60 percent

Birth rate: more than twice the national average (29 per 1,000, compared to 12 per 1,000 in Canada as a whole)

Number of communities: 28 (Iqaluit is the largest)

Most northern community: Grise Fiord (population 130), which has 24 hours of daylight every day in June, and round-the-clock darkness in December

Length of winter: 9 months

Average January temperature: –30 degrees Celsius

Average July temperature: 15 degrees Celsius

Cost of living: 1.6 to 3 times that of southern Canadians

Average household income: $31,471 (compared to $45,251 for Canada as a whole)

Number of hospitals: 1 (in Iqaluit) and 26 health centers with nursing care to serve outlying communities

bringing their craftwork with them to sell to the tourists who visit Iqaluit. These visitors are willing to pay good money for the traditional soapstone carvings. When the young adults are not busy carving, they can earn money working in the construction business, for Iqaluit has many new buildings being built.

If you are to understand Nunavut, however, you need to make a trip outside the capital. In the winter, when the snow is deeper, you might take a dogsled or a snowmobile, but in November, the bare ground

Young Inuit with a sculpture for sale

Snowmobiles provide transportation in Nunavut.

Handmade artwork

The tiny town of Kimmirut

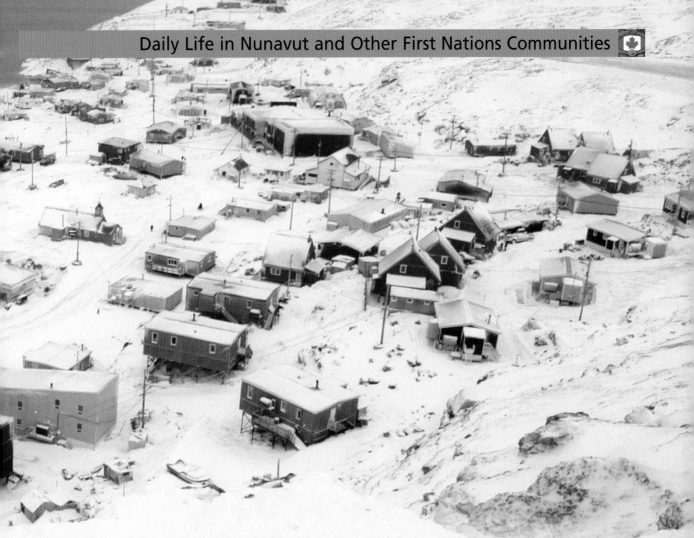

still shows in patches through the snow. The only way to get to a small town like Kimmirut is to fly.

Planes that travel between Iqaluit and outlying villages are very small, built to take off and land on the towns' short runways. You might find the plane ride rather fright-ening, as the wind that funnels between the mountains will bounce the small twin-en-gine in stomach-jerking drops and leaps until you finally touch down on Kimmirut's frozen runway.

Kimmirut has only fifty or so buildings clustered along the water's edge. At the cen-

51

Ptarmigans are wild grouse with feather-covered feet found in cold or mountainous regions.

ter of the village is the school and the co-op, a sort of general store where people can buy necessities. About four hundred people call this place home. The town gets very few tourists, but people are friendly and sometimes offer their homes to visitors. Not everyone speaks English, though, so you will need to get used to hearing Inuktitut, the Inuit native language.

What Is an Inukshuk?

Inukshuk (pronounced in-ook-shook, meaning "human image") are stone figures built by the Inuit people. In Nunavut's great wilderness, inukshuk act as compasses, guides for a safe journey. An inukshuk with two arms and legs means a valley lies ahead—and at the end of this valley, the traveler will be able to go in two directions.

These stone constructions are also spiritual symbols. They guide people across life's frozen times and give hope in barren places. What's more, inukshuk also represent the community: the hands and efforts of an entire group were required to build these massive stone sculptures. Each individual stone in an inukshuk supports and is supported by the one above and the one below it. No single piece is any more or less important than another. Its strength lies in its unity—and its significance comes from its meaning as a whole.

For supper, your hosts may offer you a meal of meat, potatoes, and bannock, a biscuit made with bits of bacon cooked in the dough. Don't be surprised, though, if your hosts choose to eat raw frozen caribou. Although the home where you stay may have many modern conveniences (like electricity, microwave ovens, and cable television), many people choose to follow the lifestyle of their ancestors—and this includes the traditional foods that come straight from the Earth.

If you take a hike outside the tiny town, you will get a sense of the surrounding land that supports these people. At first, the deep snowdrifts may hamper your steps, but as you climb higher, you'll find the snow has mostly blown away. From the vantage point of a high summit outside town, you will see for miles, from the town nestled in the little valley in front of you to the icy bay, and then across vast stretches of rocky land. Beside you, a stone inukshuk has been built on the peak, a landmark to guide travelers home.

At first glance, it seems impossible that life of any sort could survive in this barren wilderness. But if you brush aside the snow, you will find the caribou's food: lichens and moss that cling to the rocks. The caribou's gut is specially adapted to digest these tough plants. Camouflaged against the snow, rock *ptarmigans* and arctic hares scratch out seeds and frozen berries. These three animals—the caribou, rock ptarmigans, and hares—are the vital first links in Nunavut's food chain. Wolves and polar bear hunt the caribou, ptarmigan, and hares—and humans hunt the wolves and polar bear.

An inukshuk

When February comes, many of Kimmirut's residents choose to leave "civilization" in order to follow the polar bear and seals. The bear follow the seals, and the seals stay near the edge of the ice sheet that covers the water. Now that most people have snowmobiles, allowing them to cover more territory than dogsleds could, people can do as much hunting in a weekend as they once did in weeks. Hunters no longer have to stalk their prey to spear-throwing distance, since rifles allow them to take far-off animals.

If you make your way down from your high vantage point toward the center of town, you'll see many people gathered at the co-op. Inside, you find most everything for sale, from soap to salt, matches to milk. Almost everyone in town also produces some form of handcraft, and they bring their stone carvings and other crafts here to the

Christmas in Nunavut

On December 25, Santa comes to town with a gift for each person in the community. (After all, these people are practically Santa's neighbors!) The next day is the start of a two-week celebration. Each day, the regular business of life stops for several hours in the middle of the day, and the community gathers for lunch, followed by games on the ice in the harbor.

co-op, where they are shipped on for sale in Iqaluit and other places where the tourist markets are bigger. Stone sculptures bring nearly $1 million into Kimmirut annually, allowing the people here to literally "carve" themselves a living. The cost of living is extremely

Spring and Summer in Nunavut

April is the Inuit's favorite month. The days are getting longer; the snow is melting; and everyone is happy. They get out their hunting gear and get ready for the summer hunting.

During the short summer, the caribou return north, and the Inuit fill their freezers with meat. The fish swim upriver to spawn, and the waters teem with life. The bear and wolves also return, providing the Inuit with enough food and hides to last them an entire year.

Kimmirut's co-op

high, though, so nobody is getting rich (not when a quart of milk costs nearly $7.00!), but money is not a priority for the Iqaluit.

Instead, family and community are the focus of daily life. Everyone is involved in community affairs—and if one person has a need, everyone else will drop everything to help. If you go inside the school building, you will see the enormous family tree that covers an entire wall, showing the branches of relationship that connect the community.

56

A community gathering in Kimmirut is a time for laughter, games, and stories.

Even the elders join in a communal game of pick-up sticks.

Night falls early in Nunavut during November, but the community gathers together for a town meeting sponsored by the high school science class. At this meeting the elders will have a chance to share traditional time-keeping methods with the younger members of the community. Each Nunavut community has its own way of tracking the passage of time, and in Kimmirut, they use the moon. The Inuit have only begun using calendars recently; since they are an adaptable and innovative people, however, they see the advantage of using a standard calendar that allows them to communicate time concepts with the rest of the world. At the same time, however, they do not want the old ways to be eroded by modern culture. School activities are a chance for the community to pass their traditions on to the next generation.

The elders take good advantage of this opportunity, and they share many stories from their past. One elder, for example, may describe how the Inuit once made windows for their tents from caribou or seal intestines, or they may demonstrate how to create a buoy from a seal hide. After all the talk, the community enjoys a game time.

Centuries of long, cold nights forced the Inuit to come up with ways to pass the time,

An elder tells a story.

The Métis Community in Labrador

In modern-day Canada, the descendants of Native women and European men occupy and use the land throughout Labrador. They see each of their communities as being linked together in kinship and friendship. Daily life for these Métis resonates with the traditions of their elders. Their lives are built around respect for the environment, the sharing of resources, the knowledge of traditional medicines, and care for each other.

Like many First Nations, the Métis in Labrador traditionally lived their lives around the seasons. They fished and hunted seals and waterfowl in the summer months, while trapping and hunting in the forested bays and coves during the winter months. Today their relationships with the land and sea have been tested but not broken. Métis still rely on the land's resources; fish, sea mammals, birds, caribou, forests, minerals, and other natural resources are the integral elements of their daily lives. As new knowledge and modern technologies become available, though, the Métis find ways to integrate them into their traditional value systems. They see these new developments as opportunities to demonstrate their creativity and integrity as First Nations people.

The Métis of Labrador also have their own government. The Labrador Métis Association, established in 1985 and changed to the Labrador Métis Nation in 1998, is governed by an elected council comprised of four executive members and sixteen councillors.

and their innovation and love of fun inspired the creation of many games. At this community gathering, everyone plays, even the oldest and most-wrinkled elders. The hall rings with shouts and laughter as people dash back and forth playing elaborate versions of pick-up-sticks and musical chairs. Many of these people may have televisions in their homes—but they'd rather amuse themselves together, sharing laughter and fun.

The next day, the townspeople are up early, going about their business. Since the sun only shines for a few hours, people take advantage of what little daylight there is. School has been postponed, though, because there's no fresh water. A truck brings the water in every day, but today a heavy snowfall kept the truck from getting through.

As you say goodbye to Kimmirut, everyone waves and smiles, and your hosts bring you gifts. You may have only been there a

The Wendake Community in Québec

The Huron-Wendat community of Wendake, also known as Village-des-Hurons, is located on the eastern bank of the St. Charles River, five miles (8 kilometers) north of Québec City. Its land area is 277 acres (112.12 hectares). The territory contains a gravel road network (1.3 miles, 2,090 meters), a paved road network (4.7 miles, 7,510 meters), and more than five hundred houses. The Huron-Wendat have lived here for more than three hundred years. Today, they are the only Huron-Wendat community in Canada. The principal language spoken in the community is French. (Unfortunately, Huron is not spoken anymore.)

Nunavut looks ahead with hope.

62

short time, but already you feel as though you know everyone in this small, friendly town.

Back in the capital city of Iqaluit, you might be struck by the differences between this larger community and the small village of Kimmirut. In Iqaluit, people drive cars, and walk faster. Inuit and other ethnic groups keep to themselves. Government jobs draw workers from all over Canada, but these people come and go. As a result, the sense of community is not as great here as in smaller communities. The outside world comes more frequently to Iqaluit, bringing with it certain opportunities—like the Internet and other ways of connecting with pop culture—as well as problems—like drug and alcohol abuse, HIV, and other diseases.

Still, the capital city of Nunavut is a place of hope, just as the entire territory is. Visitors there have much to learn about the wisdom and spirit of Inuit culture. Grounded in the traditions of the past, the Inuit, as well as the other First Nations of Canada, look toward the future with strength and courage.

Nunavut

Five

LOOKING TOWARD THE FUTURE

Canada's First Nations have every reason to be filled with hope. More and more, they are taking their rightful place in Canada's culture and government. Their wisdom and insights are helping to guide Canada in its role in the international community. Protecting the environment is one issue where First Nations influence is most obvious.

The government of Nunavut is intensely concerned with the issues that revolve around *global warming*. It is insistent that Canada must comply with the international *Kyoto Protocol*, and it has directed all government departments to initiate energy-saving measures. The people of Nunavut have firsthand knowledge of environmental conditions that are being brought about by global warming. These changes make it more difficult for the Inuit to travel, and to have access to their resources and foods. (When winter comes later, the ice in the bays freeze later as well, which keeps the Inuit landbound, unable to go out on the ice to hunt seal and polar bear.) The Inuit are convinced that the Kyoto Protocol is vital in dealing with climate change. Their government is launching a public energy conservation campaign, and they are committed to finding alternatives to diesel fuel for generating

Global warming is the increase in the world's temperatures caused in part by the greenhouse effect and depletion of the ozone layer.

The Kyoto Protocol is a commitment among signatories to implement laws that would reduce the emission of pollutants into the air, and thereby reduce the average global temperature.

A First Nations Perspective on the Earth

"Will you ever begin to understand the meaning of the very soil beneath your feet? From a grain of sand to a great mountain, all is sacred. Yesterday and tomorrow exist eternally upon this continent. We natives are guardians of this sacred place."

electricity. These efforts on behalf of the Nunavut government act as an inspiration and a challenge, both to Canada as a whole and to the world at large.

The Northern Strategy

In 2004, Prime Minister Paul Martin and First Ministers Joseph Handley (Northwest Territories), Paul Okalik (Nunavut), and Dennis Fentie (Yukon) announced that their governments would be working together to create the first-ever comprehensive strategy for Canada's North. They would do so in co-operation with Aboriginal governments, organizations, and Northern residents.

First Minister Dennis Fentie had this to say about the Northern Strategy:

We in the North are no longer working in isolation on issues like sovereignty, on issues like the Kyoto

σ◁ᒡᖇᑐᑭᐟ ᒧᒧᑌ ᑐᑭᐟᑫᖇᒃ   Iqaluit

WELCOME TO APEX

BIENVENUE À APEX   ∆ᖅᔪ∆ᶜ

Signs in Nunavut appear in Inuktitut, English, and French.

67

Protocol and global warming. We are now working as a collective—three territories and the federal government—to address these issues. That's a significant step in the right direction.

Nunavut's first minister Paul Okalik added:

Nunavummiut have yet to attain the same social and economic standards of our fellow Canadians.

First Nations elders have much to offer.

The Northern Strategy is an opportunity for the national government to join with Nunavut in building opportunities in our unique territory that will benefit our country as a whole.

Pan-northern refers to all of the north.

First Minister Joseph Handley agreed:

We are committed to creating and following through on a vision of the North—one that will make this great region a strong, proud and contributing partner in Canada. Northerners must determine the steps for greater self-reliance in our communities. Their views must shape how we, together as territories and with the federal government, address *pan-northern* and global issues.

First Nations Perspectives on the Environment and the Future

"Today, no matter where we choose to travel, hunt, and camp, we find the traces of our ancestors. From these, we have come to understand that our life is a continuation of theirs, and we recognize that their land and culture has been given to us in trust for our children."

The Bathurst Mandate

To guide its work in Nunavut, the government has prepared a long-term plan called the Bathurst Mandate that envisions what life in Nunavut will be like in the year 2020. It outlines four major goals and guiding principles:

- *Inuuqatigiittiarniq:* Healthy Communities
- *Pijarnirniqsat Katujjiqatigiittiarnirlu:* Simplicity and Unity
- *Namminiq Makitajunnarniq:* Self-Reliance
- *Ilippallianginnarniq:* Continuing Learning

Language, the Inuit believe, is at the very heart of their cultural strength. That is why they want their government to focus on protecting and promoting Inuktitut, the territory's native language. The government of Nunavut has agreed to continue to increase the number of services provided in Inuktitut. The government will also be a workplace where more Inuktitut is spoken.

The Labrador Inuit Land Claim Agreement

Land claims are an ongoing work for First Nations groups, a work that is often slow and discouraging. Progress is being made, however, and the Inuit have finally achieved all that they have worked for.

On January 22, 2005, the Inuit of Nunatsiavut (Labrador), along with the gov-

Nunavut stop sign

70

ernments of Canada and Newfoundland and Labrador, signed the Labrador Inuit Land Claim Agreement. This agreement was the fruit of decades of work by Labrador Inuit, and it is the fourth and final such agreement for the Inuit of Canada, following claims signed in Nunavik (Northern Québec), the Inuvialuit region of the North West Territories, and Nunavut.

The Labrador Inuit first filed their claim in 1977, but not until 1990 did Canada, Newfoundland, and the Labrador Inuit Association (LIA) sign a framework agreement laying out the details of the claims negotiation process. It took another nine years of intermittent negotiations for an AIP to be signed. The Labrador AIP was ratified by the LIA membership on June 25, 2001.

Among the highlights of the AIP are that the Inuit will own and govern 6,100 square miles (15,800 square kilometers), or about 6 percent of Labrador. The LIA and the provincial government will also comanage a larger settlement area of 28,000 square miles (72,520 square kilometers). Labrador Inuit will receive 3 percent of the mining tax earned by the massive Voisey's Bay nickel-mining project. In exchange for giving up their Aboriginal title to the rest of the land, the Inuit will receive $140 million, as well as an additional $115 million to implement the final agreement.

This First Nations boy is a child of both the past and the present.

71

First Nations Economy

Many First Nations groups are working to improve their members' living conditions through small-scale projects organized at the community level. The commercial and artistic success of Inuit carving and print-making are concrete evidence of the value of this approach. Community co-ops (like the one in Kimmirut) allow communities to have more control of their economies, and educational and training programs provide

Tourism in Québec's First Nations

The Province of Québec's Société touristique des Autochtones au Québec (STAQ) represents most of the 150 Native tourist organizations in nine of Québec's ten First Nations. According to Guylaine Gill, the STAQ's general manager, the development of Native tourism offers considerable potential for the First Nations. "It makes Native people want to remain in their communities. They no longer feel isolated from the rest of the world, because the world comes to them." Tourism also creates a sense of pride within the communities. "Through tourism, Native people can teach others about their resources and lifestyles. They can also preserve and develop their culture while sharing it with others," said Ms. Gill.

Most tourist firms offer seasonal activities. Depending on the time of the year, visitors can live in the forest, sleep in tents, go hiking or snowshoeing, try their hand at dogsledding or canoeing, visit museums, and hunt or fish with Native outfitters. The STAQ is also seeking to attract school groups, offering a unique Native experience to school-age children. Native tourism has a great deal to offer adults and children alike.

both younger and older Inuit with opportunities to reshape traditional skills while acquiring the modern technical skills that help support these initiatives.

Tourism is one of the most promising economic development areas for First Nations, especially *ecotourism* and *cultural tourism*. These new industries help fuel a sense of optimism at the local and regional levels. First Nations groups hope to achieve economic self-sufficiency in a way that incorporates their cultural values.

In 1994, the Canadian Inuit Business Development Council was formally established. This council brings together all regional Inuit organizations for the purpose of promoting economic development within the broader context of Inuit culture. The objectives of this council reflect Inuit aspirations and define the potential scope of future economic activities. They are:

- to organize the members into a cooperative network to promote economic development and self-sufficiency in Inuit regions and communities.

- to develop economic cooperation, trade, and business ties among Inuit corporations and businesses, not just in Canada but in the *circumpolar* world.

- to promote Inuit employment and training opportunities in cooperative economic ventures and activities undertaken by Inuit communities, organizations, or other groups.

Ecotourism is a form of tourism that tries to minimize ecological or other damage to areas visited for their natural or cultural interest.

Cultural tourism is travel directed toward experiencing the arts, heritage, and special characteristics of a location.

Circumpolar means located or living near one or both poles of the Earth or another planet.

Nunavut is encouraging tourism.

73

Challenges Still to Be Faced

First Nations face the future with optimism—but they still have many challenges to overcome. One of the greatest is prejudice or cynicism on the part of non-Aboriginal Canadians.

According to a 2003 survey quoted by Bill Curry of the CanWest News Service, nearly half of all Canadians believe "few or none" of the hundreds of land claims made by First Nations groups are valid. A full 49 percent of Canadians take issue with the validity of Aboriginal land claims, says the poll of 3,204 Canadians by the Centre for Research and Information on Canada, compared with 45 percent who said "all or many" land claims are valid. The poll also found that 42 percent of Canadians believe it would be better to do away with Aboriginal treaty rights and "treat Aboriginal people the same as other Canadians." On the specific issue of hunting and fishing rights, 63 percent of the people who responded to the poll said natural resources should be regulated in such a way that everyone is treated the same; only 35 percent supported the idea that Aboriginal peoples should have preferential access to hunting and fishing grounds in areas where they have traditionally lived.

Nancy Pine, a spokeswoman for the Assembly of First Nations chief Phil Fontaine, said the poll showed the need for more public education about treaty rights. "Without a proper understanding," she said, "this may create unfounded fear or discomfort with the implications of claims or initiatives, so it really does point to a need for greater public education, more dialogue between First Nations and non-aboriginal people." Andrew Parkin, the codirector

Land Claim Progress

Since 1974, the federal government has settled 254 land claims worth a total of $1.7 billion. However, hundreds more have yet to be resolved.

of the survey, agreed that the results show a need for more education:

> There's a significant body of opinion that is out of sync with the constitutional reality of this country. Treaty rights, land rights and even self-government have been **constitutionalized** since 1982 and have been repeatedly upheld by the courts.

While this survey found that many Canadians are uneasy about Aboriginal rights, it also found that three out of every

*Something that is **constitutionalized** has been authorized through a constitution.*

IQALUIT

75

Nunavut woman connects the past and the present

four Canadians think it is beneficial to the entire nation that First Nations' distinctive cultures remain strong. In general, the poll shows Canadians believe relations between Aboriginal peoples and other Canadians are improving—and they recognize the vital role this group plays in their national identity.

The Royal Commission on Aboriginal Peoples claims that the relationship between First Nations and the newcomers has four distinct *evolutionary* phases: separate worlds, contact and cooperation, displacement and assimilation, and negotiation and renewal. The people of Canada have worked their way through the first three stages. Now comes the hard work of negotiation and renewal.

Writers Radwanski and Luttrell, authors of *The Will of a Nation: Awakening the Canadian Spirit*, summarize the role of the First Nations groups in Canada's history and present reality:

> We have come perilously close to destroying an entire people. It is a testament to the strength of the aboriginal nations and their culture that they have not been broken or assimilated despite all they have endured. But they have paid, and are still paying today, a terrible price for their determination to hold on to their identity. . . .

We cannot undo all the harm that was done in the past. But we cannot be the nation we want to be unless we do everything in our power to ensure justice for aboriginal Canadians in the present and the future.

Evolutionary *means developing in small increments that accumulate to bring about significant change.*

Nunavut child

First Nations inukshuk is a symbol of hope.

77

1492 Christopher Columbus arrives in the Americas.

1985 The Labrador Métis Association is established; name changed to Labrador Métis Nation in 1998.

1876 Canadian government passes the Indian Act.

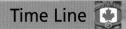

Summer 1991 Mohawk Indians declare war over rejected land claims.

1990 Canadian government signs an agreement in principle with the Tungavik Federation of Nunavut and the government of the Northwest Territories.

May 25, 1993 Nunavut Land Claims Agreement is signed.

April 1, 1999 Nunavut becomes
Canada's newest and largest territory.

June 25, 2001 Labrador Inuit Association
ratifies the agreement in principle for
land claims negotiations.

January 22, 2005 Inuit of Nunatsiavut (Labrador) and governments of Canada and Newfoundland and Labrador sign the Labrador Inuit Land Claim Agreement.

February 16, 2005 Kyoto Protocol goes into effect.

FURTHER READING

Beckett, Harry. *Nunavut*. New York: Weigl, 2003.

Dickason, Olive Patricia. *Canada's First Nations: A History of Founding Peoples from Earliest Times*. New York: Oxford, 2001.

Hancock, Lyn. *Nunavut*. New York: Lerner, 1995.

Quan, Holly. *Native Chiefs and Famous Métis*. Toronto, Ont.: Altitude, 2003.

Sealey, D. Bruce. *Metis: Canada's Forgotten People*. Toronto, Ont.: Pemmican, 2000.

Sharp, Anne Wallace. *The Inuit*. San Diego, Calif.: Lucent, 2002.

FOR MORE INFORMATION

About Nunavut
npc.nunavut.ca/eng/nunavut/

City of Iqaluit
www.city.iqaluit.nu.ca

Kyoto Protocol
unfccc.int/resource/docs/convkp/
kpeng.html

Nunatsiaq News (Nunavut Territory
newspaper)
www.nunatsiaq.com

Nunavut Handbook
www.nunavuthandbook.com

Nunavut Land Claims Agreement Act
laws.justice.gc.ca/en/N-28.7

Nunavut Land Claims issues
www.polarnet.ca/polarnet.ca/polarnet/
nunavut.htm

Nunavut tourism
www.nunavuttourism.com

Publisher's note:
The Web sites listed on this page were active at the time of publication. The publisher is not responsible for Web sites that have changed their addresses or discontinued operation since the date of publication. The publisher will review and update the Web-site list upon each reprint.

INDEX

PICTURE CREDITS

Benjamin Stewart, hardinghousegraphics@stny.rr.com: pp. 1, 8, 11, 12, 15, 16, 17, 18–19, 21, 22–23, 24, 25, 29, 30, 31, 32–33, 34, 36–37, 38, 39, 43 (right), 44, 46, 48, 49, 50–51, 53, 54–55, 56, 57, 58, 59, 62, 64–65, 66–67, 68, 70, 71, 73, 74–75, 76, 78–79, 80–81

Howe's Cavern Iroquois Indian Museum: p. 26

BIOGRAPHIES
AUTHORS AND PHOTOGRAPHER

Ellyn Sanna, editor in chief of Harding House Publishing Service, has written many fiction and nonfiction books for both children and adults. She is proud to claim a First Nations ancestor (Iroquois) as part of her family heritage. William Hunter and Benjamin Stewart, this book's coauthor and photographer, traveled to Nunavut to do the research and take the photographs for this book. They are grateful to all the First Nations people who welcomed them and willingly shared their lives and culture.

SERIES CONSULTANT

Dr. David Bercuson is the Director of the Centre for Military and Strategic Studies at the University of Calgary. His writings on modern Canadian politics, Canadian defense and foreign policy, and Canadian military, among other topics, have appeared in academic and popular publications. Dr. Bercuson is the author, coauthor, or editor of more than thirty books, including *Confrontation at Winnipeg: Labour, Industrial Relations, and the General Strike* (1990), *Colonies: Canada to 1867* (1992), *Maple Leaf Against the Axis, Canada's Second World War* (1995), and *Christmas in Washington: Roosevelt and Churchill Forge the Alliance* (2005). He has also served as historical consultant for several film and television projects, and provided political commentary for CBC radio and television and CTV television. In 1989, Dr. Bercuson was elected a fellow of the Royal Society of Canada. In 2004, Dr. Bercuson received the Vimy Award, sponsored by the Conference of Defence Association Institute, in recognition of his significant contributions to Canada's defense and the preservation of the Canadian democratic principles.